CALAMITY JANE
FRONTIER ORIGINAL

William R. Sanford &
Carl R. Green

Enslow Publishers, Inc.

40 Industrial Road	PO Box 38
Box 398	Aldershot
Berkeley Heights, NJ 07922	Hants GU12 6BP
USA	UK

http://www.enslow.com

Library of Congress Cataloging-in-Publication Data

Sanford, William R. (William Reynolds), 1927–
    Calamity Jane : frontier original / by William R. Sanford and Carl R. Green.
       p. cm. — (Legendary heroes of the Wild West)
    ISBN 0-89490-647-X
    1. Calamity Jane, 1852–1903—Juvenile literature. 2. Women pioneers—
West (U.S.)—Biography—Juvenile literature. 3. Pioneers—West (U.S.)—
Biography—Juvenile literature. 4. West (U.S.) —Biography—Juvenile literature.
I. Green, Carl R. II. Title. III. Series: Sanford, William R. (William Reynolds),
1927–   Legendary heroes of the Wild West.
F594.C2S26 1996
978'.02'092—dc20
[B]   95-41420
                                          CIP
                                          AC

Printed in the United States of America

10 9 8 7

Illustration Credits: Centennial Archives, Deadwood Public Library, Deadwood, South Dakota, pp. 23, 28; Denver Public Library, Western History Collection, pp. 6, 15, 18, 22, 26, 33, 37; Library of Congress, pp. 14, 19, 39, 41; William R. Sanford and Carl R. Green, pp. 7, 11, 12, 31, 35.

Cover Illustration: Paul Daly

CONTENTS

AUTHORS' NOTE

The Wild West was mostly a man's world. A woman had to be colorful, tough, and sure of herself to share center stage with the legendary male heroes. One of the women who accomplished that feat was Martha Cannary. Most people know this remarkable woman by her more colorful nickname—Calamity Jane. In her lifetime Calamity Jane rode, shot, drank, and cussed with the best of 'em. Dozens of dime novels claimed to tell her story. In modern times, she has been given new life in films and on television. Most of the stories told about her stray far from the truth. That's too bad, because the real story of Calamity Jane is just as exciting. This book tells her true story.

1

WHO WAS THE REAL CALAMITY JANE?

T he Wild West vanished in the early 1900s. Today it exists only in books, on film, and in the hearts of people the world over. Each year, tourists fan out across the West, drawn by that fabled era. They visit towns with names like Leadville and Tombstone. In South Dakota, they flock to the old mining town of Deadwood.

Two western legends lie in Deadwood's cemetery. An iron fence guards the grave of lawman Wild Bill Hickok. Close by, a tombstone marks the resting place of Calamity Jane.

A few visitors doubt that Calamity Jane was real. The tombstone is a fake, they say, put up to draw tourists. Others say they have no doubts at all. Calamity's life, they point out, touched too many people to be anything but real. Are all of the stories told about her true? Calamity's death in 1903 left more questions than answers.

What was Calamity's real name? Calamity lies under a tombstone marked "Mrs. M. E. Burke." The "M" stands for Martha. Calamity herself wrote, "My maiden name was Marthy Cannary."[1] The name "Burke" comes from the last of her husbands. No one knows what the "E" stands for. That leaves the "Jane" in Calamity Jane to puzzle us. The best guess is that her parents named her Martha Jane. If not, Calamity may have given herself a middle name. Another guess is that it could have been a slang term for "girl." In the 1800s men used "jane" the way some people use "babe" or "honey" today.

When and where was Calamity born? Martha Cannary's birth records have vanished. Researchers must

work from the slimmest of clues. One group is certain she was born Jane Dalton in 1860. They say her father was a soldier at Fort Laramie, Wyoming.[2] A second group argues that Calamity was born in Burlington, Iowa. Her

The Wild West knew her as Calamity Jane. That was the name Martha Cannary preferred. The real life Calamity could outride and outshoot most of the women—and many of the men—of her day.

In the Wild West, cowboys and miners could go months without seeing a woman. When a woman did arrive in town, she was guaranteed a warm welcome. That fact, combined with her generous personality, helps account for Calamity Jane's popularity.

father, they insist, was a Baptist preacher.[3] Perhaps we should let Calamity have the last word. She wrote that she was born in Princeton, Missouri, on May 1, 1852. An 1864 newspaper story supports that date. It locates a twelve-year-old girl named "Canary" in Montana in 1864.[4]

What did Calamity look like? Movie fans tend to think of Calamity in terms of the women who have played her on the screen. They may remember her as a blonde Doris Day or a tight-lipped Anjelica Houston. The truth was less glamorous. An early photo of Calamity shows a strong, lean, dark-haired woman of twenty-three. Later photos reveal that she put on weight as she aged. When it comes to details, the experts differ. Some say her hair was a copper-red when she was young.[5] Others describe her hair as "raven" (black).

One old-timer who knew her said she was six feet tall and brown-eyed. A reporter of the time did not agree. He called her "a small creature." Experts agree that the young Calamity was lively and high-spirited. Some add that she was a beauty. If she was, hard living in a harsh climate changed her. One observer went so far as to say, "She was real tall and built like a busted bale of hay."[6]

Why are there so many Calamity Jane stories? One woman could not have done all that Calamity is supposed to have done. Because she was famous, others copied her name and style. In time, any western woman who wore men's clothing was called a Calamity Jane. In 1877, a woman in Cheyenne, Wyoming, paid a $10 fine for dressing like a man. Cheyenne also had its own Calamity Sal. In Denver, a local drunk named Mattie Young was sometimes known as "Calamity Jane."[7] No one who knew Martha Cannary confused these women with the real thing.

So, forget the legends and the Hollywood image. Here's the true story of the one and only Calamity Jane.

2
GROWING UP
WILD AND FREE

Martha Cannary Burke wrote that she was born on May 1, 1852. The place was Princeton, Missouri, a town near the Iowa border. Charlotte and Robert Cannary named their first child Martha. Their pet name for her was Marthy. As the years passed, Charlotte gave birth to five more children.

The Cannarys lived in a cabin that Robert built. He raised corn in fields that his father had cleared. Money was scarce. As Martha grew up, she helped take care of the younger children. No one knows how much schooling she had—if any.

The Cannarys were less than perfect parents. Robert liked to drink whiskey. Red-haired Charlotte flirted with the local men. Years later, a neighbor remembered twelve-year-old Martha. The girl was "wild as a lynx kitten," she said.[1] Thanks to Charlotte, Martha could outcuss most men. Her passions were horses and the outdoors. "I became an expert rider, being able to ride the most vicious and stubborn of horses," she wrote.[2]

In the 1850s, the debate over slavery turned violent. Raiders from Kansas burned and looted Missouri's border region. In 1861, the nation plunged into the Civil War. Although Missouri was a slave state, it stayed in the Union. Armies from the North and South turned its fertile fields into a battleground. In 1864, with the war raging on, the Cannarys left the state.

Robert Cannary drove a wagon southwest to Independence. The bustling town on the Missouri River was the starting point of the western trails. Ahead lay the Great Plains. Martha had always longed for adventure. The trip must have been a dream come true.

The Cannarys hooked up with a wagon train. To travel alone was to invite attack by hostile bands of Native Americans. Slow-moving oxen hauled the wagons along the rutted Oregon Trail. On many days a wagon train covered as little as seven miles.

Women and girls wore long dresses and sunbonnets. They rode in the wagons or walked beside the oxen. Martha would have none of that. She spent her days in the saddle. "I was at all times with the men when there was excitement and adventures to be had," she wrote. She also bragged that the hunters thought she was a good shot and a fearless rider.[3] The women could only mutter and shake their heads. They were outraged at the sight of a girl who dressed and rode like a boy.

Five months later, the Cannarys left the Oregon Trail.

In 1864, the Cannary family headed west with a wagon train. It was a time of high adventure for twelve-year-old Martha Jane Cannary. In this engraving, she could have been one of the riders driving horses into the circle of wagons. Women would have been outraged to see her dressing like a man and doing a "man's work."

Robert had heard that gold had been discovered in Montana. The route that led across the mountains was hard going. The men had to use ropes to lower the wagons down steep slopes. Quicksand sucked at the oxen's hooves as the wagons splashed through boggy stream crossings. Heavy rains raised rivers to the flood stage. A strong current almost swept Martha away.

The Cannarys rolled at last into a rough mining camp called Virginia City. The settlement was the center of the mining claims that lined Alder Gulch. Robert tried his hand at mining and then turned to gambling. Charlotte was forced to take in washing. In December 1864, the local paper mentioned the family. The report described three little girls named "Canary" who were seen begging from door to door.[4]

Charlotte died of pneumonia in 1866. Robert moved the children to Utah that spring, and died there a year later. A Mormon family took in the younger Cannarys. Martha and the older children soon drifted on to Fort Bridger, Wyoming. She dated their arrival as May 1, 1868—her sixteenth birthday.[5] That was the last time her autobiography mentions her brothers and sisters.

For a while, Martha earned her keep by cooking and washing clothes. After her life on the trail, "women's work" must have bored her.

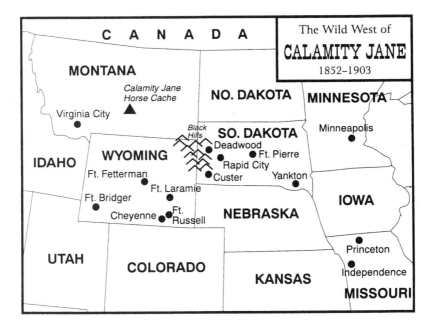

Calamity Jane's careers as muleskinner, scout, nurse, and entertainer took her through most of the territory shown on this map. It was in the Black Hills mining town of Deadwood that she first came to public attention.

3

A NEW LIFE AND A COLORFUL NICKNAME

Martha Cannary found the excitement she craved in Wyoming. In Piedmont, she met the men who laid track for the Union Pacific. Mile by mile, they were racing to meet the Central Pacific in Utah. When the tracks met, the nation would be spanned by rails from sea to sea.

A foreman hired Martha as a bullwacker. Her job was to drive the ox teams that pulled the supply wagons. A twenty-foot whip kept the oxen moving. Later, Martha boasted that she could "pick a fly off [an] oxen's ear four times out of five."[1] At night, the teenager's tall tales made the workmen laugh. They bought her drinks to keep the stories coming.

Drinking and cussing were not Martha's only vices. She may have loved too many men too well. A U.S. marshal called her a "camp follower," a woman who hung around work camps and army forts. Martha's stay in

One of Calamity's first jobs as a teenager was driving ox teams like the one shown here. She quickly learned to handle the twenty-foot whip used to control the slow-moving oxen. She also learned to drink and cuss like her fellow bullwackers.

Cheyenne lasted only a few days. A local lawman ordered her to leave.[2]

Martha's movements during this time are hard to trace. Some reports say she married a man named Washburn. It is almost certain that she cut her hair short and wore pants. She wrote that she went to Fort Russell, Wyoming, in 1870. There she claimed to have hired on as a scout for General George Custer. When Custer left for Arizona, she said, he took her along. She wrote: "When I joined Custer, I donned the uniform of a soldier. It was a bit awkward [but] . . . I soon got to be perfectly at home in men's clothes."[3]

Research finds a few faults in this account. Custer never served at Fort Russell, nor did he lead soldiers into Arizona. In 1870, he was in Kansas writing his *War Memoirs*. Martha also wrote that she was ordered to Fort

Custer in 1874. That fort, it turns out, was not built until 1878.

Was she the Wild West's grandest liar? Not really. It was an age of tall tales. If a tale lacked color, the storyteller added bigger and better "facts." Martha told the story of her life in that spirit. She did not dream that someday each date and place would be checked and cross-checked.

By 1872, Martha was better known as Calamity Jane. She claimed that a Captain Egan had given her the nickname. The story began with a troop of soldiers who were ambushed by Native Americans. Martha rescued the wounded captain and carried him to safety. When he recovered, Egan told her, "I name you Calamity Jane, the heroine of the plains."[4]

Egan denied the story, but it survived. Martha loved her new name. When she entered a saloon she liked to shout, "I'm Calamity Jane and the drinks are on me!"[5]

In the spring of 1875,

Calamity Jane claimed that she earned her famous nickname while serving as a U.S. Army scout. This old photo shows her armed with a rifle and dressed for a scouting assignment with General George Crook. Did she narrowly escape death with General Custer at the Little Bighorn? Calamity seldom let the truth interfere with a good story.

U.S. Army troops rode into the Black Hills of South Dakota. By treaty, the region belonged to the Sioux "for as long as the grass shall grow." When gold was discovered, treaties were forgotten. The army sent four hundred troops to protect white miners and settlers.

Colonel R. I. Dodge refused Calamity's request to go along. That did not stop her. She pretended to be a man, put on a uniform, and marched with the troops. One story says her boyfriend, Sergeant Frank Siechrist, helped her. She was found out one hot day when the men went swimming. Calamity stripped off her uniform and joined them. When an officer spotted her, he took the news to the colonel. Dodge sent the fake private back to Fort Laramie.[6]

Early in 1876, the army went to war against the Sioux. Calamity claimed that General George Crook took her along as a scout. More likely, Crook hired her as a wagon driver. Calamity also claimed a narrow escape at the Little Bighorn. A ride to Fort Fetterman with dispatches saved her. During the ninety-mile ride, she became chilled after fording a river. Instead of riding with the doomed Custer, she ended up in the hospital.[7]

Back on her feet, Calamity moved on to Fort Laramie. While she was there, she met Wild Bill Hickok.

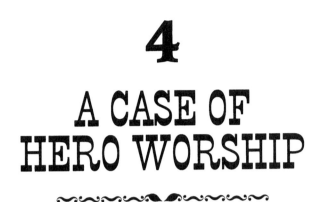

4

A CASE OF HERO WORSHIP

John Pearson struck pay dirt in Deadwood Gulch, South Dakota, in 1876. News of the strike soon drew twenty-five thousand miners to the Black Hills. Calamity joined the gold rush late in June. Wild Bill Hickok and some of his friends rode with her.

The party made a grand entrance. Calamity was mounted on a black horse named Satan. She wore a white buckskin suit and a ten-gallon hat. Both horse and outfit were gifts from Wild Bill. Bill was just as splendid in fringed buckskins and a white Stetson.[1]

Miners whooped a warm welcome. Old friends bought drinks for Calamity as she swaggered from bar to bar. When a barkeeper told her to quiet down, she shot out a mirror with her six-gun. Men lined up to join the game when Wild Bill sat down to play cards. Most did not care if they won or lost. They wanted to brag that they had played poker with Wild Bill Hickok.

After the free drinks ran out, Calamity went to work. She wrote later that she carried the mail between the towns of Deadwood and Custer. Some experts doubt her story, but no one doubts her skill as a rider. The hundred-mile round trip, she said, took her through outlaw country. No one tried to stop her. The "toll collectors," as she called the outlaws, thought she was a "good fellow." They also knew that she could handle a pistol.[2]

Once in a while Calamity let her heart rule her head. In July the local paper reported, "The man, Warren, who was stabbed on lower Main Street . . . is doing quite well under the care of Calamity Jane. . . . She is deserving of much praise."[3]

Men were drawn to this softer side of Calamity Jane. During her lifetime, she claimed to have been married ten or more times.

Wild Bill Hickok was the great love of Calamity Jane's life. She went to her grave insisting that she was married to the handsome lawman. Equally hard to confirm is her claim that she gave birth to Wild Bill's child. If Wild Bill was romantically involved with Calamity Jane, he kept his feelings well-hidden.

Deadwood blossomed almost overnight after miners found gold in South Dakota's Black Hills. Calamity caught her first glimpse of the ramshackle main street when she rode into town with Wild Bill Hickok. The lively nightlife of the town was much to her liking. After Wild Bill's death, she found work as a bartender and stayed on.

One year she called herself "Mrs. Dorsett." A year or two later she was "Mrs. Dalton." The records add names like Somers, Hunt, Steers, Townley, and King. Except for her 1885 wedding to Charlie Burke, her "marriages" did not last. The man Calamity wanted most was beyond her reach.

Years later, Calamity claimed that Wild Bill Hickok had married her on the trip to the Black Hills. No one knows how Wild Bill felt about her. He seemed amused when she tagged after him. If he did marry her, those spur-of-the-moment vows left Bill saddled with one wife too many. He was already married to Agnes Lake, a circus owner.

On August 2, 1876, fate took a hand in the game. Wild Bill was playing poker in the Number 10 Saloon that day. A gunman named Jack McCall slipped in and shot Bill in the head. Bill died with two aces and two eights in his hand. Poker players still call that "the Dead Man's Hand."

Calamity heard the news soon after the shooting. As she told the story, "I at once started to look for the assassin. [I] found him at Shurdy's butcher shop. [Grabbing] a meat cleaver [I] made him throw up his hands." She then described the killer's escape and recapture. McCall, she wrote, was later put on trial and hung in Yankton, South Dakota.[4]

It makes a grand story, but it is one of Calamity's tall tales. McCall was captured without her aid. Instead of escaping, he was turned loose by a miners' court. The jurors believed him when he said Wild Bill had killed his brother. Only the fact that he was tried again and hung in Yankton is true.

Calamity stayed on in Deadwood, working as a bartender. The sight shocked the more proper townswomen. The men would not help, so the women made their own plans. As Calamity told the story, the women stomped into the saloon with a horsewhip and shears. Clearly, they were there to cut off the rest of her hair. "I jumped off the bar into their midst," she wrote. "Before they could say 'sickem' I had them bowling."[5] The women retreated and Calamity went back to work.

Two years later, smallpox struck in Deadwood. The outbreak brought out the best in Calamity.

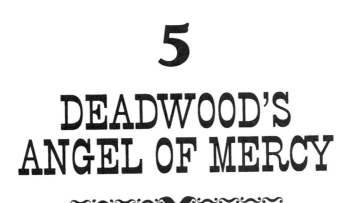

5

DEADWOOD'S
ANGEL OF MERCY

Fact and fiction often mix in Calamity Jane's story. On one event, almost everyone agrees. Smallpox hit the Black Hills with stunning force in 1878. With sick and dying men all around her, Calamity became a nurse.

Smallpox came to the Americas with the first European settlers. Once ashore, it spread like wildfire. In time, the disease killed over half of the Native American population. The people of Deadwood, however, need not have suffered. Eighty years earlier, Edward Jenner had developed a smallpox vaccine in England. The vaccine was little used in the Wild West. Indeed, medicines of any kind were in short supply. Smallpox was only one of the diseases that raged through the mining towns.

Hundreds fell ill in Deadwood, and many died. Calamity watched as eight smallpox victims were carried to a cabin above Spruce Gulch. Fearful of catching the disease, the other miners shunned the cabin. When the doctor paid a visit, he found Calamity there. Her pockmarked face proved that she had survived her own battle with smallpox. "You just tell me what to do, Doc, and I'll do it," she told him.[1]

Calamity cared for the miners around the clock. When supplies ran low, she went to the general store. Calmly, she filled a burlap sack with food. The storekeeper told her that the cost was two ounces of gold. Hearing that, Calamity drew her pistol. "I'm Calamity Jane, by God, and them sick boys I'm lookin' out for up in the hills don't

pay for no grub till they get good and able." The storekeeper knew better than to argue. He watched in silence as she backed out the door.[2] From that day on, merchants chipped in with free food and blankets.

Miners panned for gold in the streambed below the cabin. To save time, Calamity yelled at them when she needed something. One of the miners

Although she usually dressed in men's clothing, Calamity was no stranger to women's wear.

Calamity's tough talk and swagger concealed a soft heart. If a miner's family was in trouble, she could be counted on to bring aid and comfort. She was especially tender with the children who worked beside their parents in the streams and mines around Deadwood.

would make the trip to the general store. When the man returned, Calamity pulled the supplies up on a rope. She also hauled up buckets of water to fill the barrel behind the cabin. Soon she had a line of washing flapping in the wind.

If Calamity was an angel of mercy, she was a rough one. While bathing a dying miner, she might snap, "It ain't time for you to conk out, pard." To ease the pain, she added cream of tartar and Epsom salts to the water. Neither had any healing value. Three of the men died. Calamity wrapped each body in a blanket. As her other patients looked on, she recited, "Now I lay me down to sleep." It was the only prayer she knew.[3] That duty done, she yelled down to the miners, "Dig a hole." When the grave was ready, she carried each body to the site. Then she shoveled dirt into the hole.

Calamity made sure that her patients received food, drink, and clean clothes. Thanks to her tireless care, five of them survived. One of the men told her he longed to return to his family in the East. When she learned that he was broke, Calamity knew what to do. She started her campaign outside a Main Street saloon. A crowd gathered when she climbed atop a beer barrel. "Untie your weasel skins and turn out enough dust to take him back where he belongs," she yelled. The gold dust she collected in her hat paid for the man's train ticket home.[4]

Hard times seemed to bring out the best in Calamity. With the cabin empty of patients, she visited the sick all along the gulch. At each stop she delivered food, drink, and comfort. Sick children saw through her gruff ways. She cuddled them and kept them amused with her tall tales. Years later, grown to adulthood, they still treasured her kindness.

6
FOOTLOOSE IN THE OLD WEST

Deadwood was Calamity's home, but she was too footloose to stay there. When the smallpox epidemic was over, she moved on. In 1878, she spent some time looking for gold. For someone who craved carefree drinking partners, it must have been a lonely life.

Calamity turned up a year later in Rapid City. Once again she found work as a bullwacker. She wrote: "In 1879 I . . . drove teams from Rapid City to Fort Pierre. . . . This teaming was done with oxen as they were better fitted for the work than horses."[1]

The last statement tells us Calamity's thoughts in an old debate. Which animal was better for hauling heavy loads—horses or oxen? Without a doubt, horses were faster. On the minus side, they broke down under heavy loads. They also had to be fed grain, which was in short supply. Oxen were at their best pulling heavy loads across rough country. They were slow but steady, and they cost less. Oxen were lifesavers, too, when a wagon train was attacked. To a Native American, a good riding horse was worth a dozen oxen.

On the trail, Calamity walked next to her freight wagon, whip in hand. The wagons were built without seats. The only place to ride, sitting or standing, was on

This old photograph, taken in Denver, identifies the smiling, well-dressed woman as Calamity Jane. She is flanked by two mountain men—C.S. Stobie (left) and Jack Crawford. If the woman is Calamity, the photo was taken when she was still young and slender. In later photos, as one onlooker remarked, her figure looks more like a "busted bale of hay."

the wagon tongue. In dry weather, clouds of dust choked the drivers. Calamity wore a bandanna across her face, but still the dust stung her eyes. When it rained, she sloshed through rivers of mud. Men who saw her said she looked at least forty-five. No one would have believed she was not yet thirty.[2]

The 150-mile trip from Fort Pierre to Rapid City took three weeks. In summer, Calamity had her team moving by four A.M. At eight o'clock, the wagon train stopped for a long break. Pushing ahead during the hottest part of the day wore out both oxen and drivers. At four o'clock, the whips cracked again, driving the oxen on for another four hours. When night fell, the bullwackers gathered near a campfire to eat, drink, and tell stories. Calamity, with her vast store of tall tales, was a popular member of the noisy crew. By ten o'clock, the bullwackers all were asleep under their wagons.

Calamity was as good a driver as she was a storyteller. Urging the slow-witted animals on with a string of curses was second nature to her. The rawhide whip, expertly cracked over the oxen's heads, kept them moving. Cracking a whip for hours at a time took strength and endurance. Calamity had both.

Bullwacking paid a dollar a day plus grub. By 1882, Calamity was ready to try an easier job. At Fort Pierre, she exchanged her soiled buckskins for an old pink gown. In her new outfit, she embarked on a brief new career as a midwife. A woman about to give birth would call for Calamity. If the woman could not pay, Calamity helped deliver the baby for free. When children ran underfoot, she sat them in a corner. Once seated, the little ones did not dare stray.[3]

Later that year, Calamity wrote, she bought a ranch on the Yellowstone. If she did so, the money must have come from her mining claims. To bring in extra money, she also opened an inn. It was a place, she wrote, "where the weary traveler could [find] food, drink, or trouble if he looked

Calamity could always find work as a bullwacker. In 1879, she drove ox teams from Rapid City to Fort Pierre. The 150-mile trip took three weeks, and paid a dollar a day. This photo shows an ox team plodding slowly through Deadwood. The street has yet to be paved, but progress shows in the telegraph lines strung on the pole at the left.

for it."[4] During this time, she was thrown out of a dance hall for making a tenderfoot "dance." The trick was to shoot close to the man's toes without hitting them. On another night, she leaned out of a hotel window to curse a stingy customer. A crowd gathered to cheer her long, expert performance.[5]

By 1883, Calamity was on the move again. Over the next year or two, she visited Oregon, California, and Arizona. No matter where she went, her fame was there first. Some eastern writers had seen to that.

7

"THE HEROINE OF WHOOP-UP"

Left on her own, Calamity might have lived and died with little notice. Her fame grew because eastern writers featured her in their Wild West stories. She was an instant hit with readers. Who could resist such a colorful nickname? Calamity herself retold the stories as if they were true. She did reject a report that called her a "horse thief" and a "minister's daughter." Both statements were false, she swore.[1]

Writer Ned Wheeler pushed Calamity into the spotlight in 1877. Wheeler never met Calamity, nor did he know much about the West. Born in New York, he lived and died in Pennsylvania. To make up for his lack of knowledge, he relied on news reports. To hold his readers, he added shocking details and tricky plots. He could—and did—turn a simple card game into a life-and-death drama.

His stories appeared in weekly magazines called dime novels.

At first Calamity Jane played only a minor role in Wheeler's stories. The hero's role went to an outlaw called Deadwood Dick. The public loved the stories and begged for more. Calamity emerged as Dick's sidekick. One popular title was "Deadwood Dick on Deck; or, Calamity Jane, the Heroine of Whoop-Up." The cover featured a drawing of Calamity.

In Wheeler's stories, Calamity was brave, bright, and beautiful. She dressed in buckskins and a mink-fringed vest. Her long hair was a glossy black, her eyes "black and piercing." This make-believe Calamity saved Dick's life a number of times. In one story, she helped him avoid hanging. In another, she rescued him from a mine explosion. Wheeler's writing style was typical of his day. In this scene, Calamity arrives just as the villain slashes Dick with a knife:

Ned Wheeler never traveled further west than Pennsylvania. He never met Calamity Jane. These handicaps did not stop him from writing popular stories set in the Wild West. Wheeler based his tales on news reports, but the plots, descriptions, and dialogue were his own invention.

"You vile varmint," cried Calamity Jane, pulling the hammer of one of her revolvers back to full cock. "You cursed fool. Don't you know that that only seals yer own miserable fate?"

"Don't shoot, Jennie!" [Dick] gasped, the blood spurting from his wound. "This ain't none o' your funeral. . . . Take me to the cab—"

He could not finish the sentence. A sickening stream of blood gushed from his mouth, and he fell back upon the ground. [A whistle brings Dick's gang to his aid.]

"Seize these two cusses and guard 'em well!" Calamity said, grimly. . . . "In a few days, no doubt, you'll have the pleasure of attending their funerals."[2]

Newspapers did not lag far behind the dime novels. Editors knew their readers enjoyed stories like this one:

This was in the cow town of Oakes, North Dakota. [Calamity] drank much and in one saloon the cowboys began to [tease] her. Calamity Jane smiled grimly and asked everyone up to the bar. They howled. Two revolvers suddenly appeared in the woman's hands. She could draw as quickly as any man who ever lived.

"Dance, you tenderfeet, dance," she commanded grimly, and fired a few shots by way of emphasis.

They danced, and with much vigor.[3]

The real-life Calamity did have a temper. The editor of the *Cheyenne Daily Leader* claimed that she once stormed into his office with a horsewhip. He fled when she cracked the whip over his head. When he returned, the office was in a shambles. A note was tacked to the door. It read: "Print in the *Leader* that Calamity Jane . . . is in Cheyenne, or I'll scalp you, skin you alive and hang you to a telegraph pole. You hear me, and don't you forget it. *Calamity Jane.*"[4]

In another story, Calamity rode her horse into a saloon. Asked why, she explained that the horse wanted to dance. Are these stories true? No one knows for sure. Calamity probably did say to a cowboy friend: "I want to be left alone to go to Hell in my own way. I want to be with you boys, that's the only life I know."[5]

Calamity Jane, for all her colorful exploits, would have died an unknown but for the dime novel. An eastern writer, Ned Wheeler, propelled her to fame by writing her into his Deadwood Dick stories. As this Pocket Library cover indicates, the fictional Calamity was a dashing, glamorous heroine.

8

A BRIEF CAREER IN SHOW BUSINESS

The dime novels brought fame, but Calamity's pockets stayed empty. In 1894, she gave up roaming and joined a rodeo at Cinnabar, Montana. The crowd loved her. She showed off her sharpshooting by plugging silver dollars. That night she rode off with a sock full of battered silver coins.[1]

A year later, Calamity was back in Deadwood. This time she was traveling with Charlie Burke, her new husband. Broke again, Calamity made some money by selling photographs of herself. The money, she claimed, was earmarked for her adopted daughter, Jessie Hickok. The ten-year-old, she said, was staying at a nearby convent school. Researchers think Jessie was most likely Burke's stepdaughter.[2]

The town threw a fund-raising dance at the Green Front Saloon. The women of Deadwood wore bloomers to the dance. The daring new garments looked like baggy trousers gathered tightly at the ankles. For once, Calamity's pants were right in style. The local paper reported, "Many there were who were anxious to spend 25¢ to dance with her. [Then they could] say they had danced with 'Calamity Jane.'" The paper went on to say that Calamity was seen smoking a "vile cigar."[3]

As the night wore on, Calamity forgot about little Jessie. She used the donations to buy drinks for the house. The fun went on until she passed out. In the morning Calamity picked up the money that was left and rode out of town. She never spoke of Jessie again. Perhaps she did use the funds to pay for the girl's schooling. The school has never released its records.[4]

In 1895, Buffalo Bill Cody was making a fortune with his Wild West Show. Two showmen named Kohl and Middleton tried to copy him. Middleton found

~~~~~~~~~~~~~~~

Ned Wheeler's stories brought fame to Calamity, but no income. In 1896, two promoters hired her for their Wild West show. Calamity's role, as advertised in this old poster, was to stand on a platform and tell stories. The money was good, but the strain of talking to noisy strangers depressed Calamity.

Kohl & Middleton's

PALACE MUSEUM

Week Beginning Monday, Jan. 20.

CALAMITY JANE!

The Famous Woman Scout of the Wild West! Heroine of a Thousand Thrilling Adventures! The Terror of Evildoers in the Black Hills! The Comrade of Buffalo Bill and Wild Bill! See this Famous Woman and Hear Her Graphic Description of Her Daring Exploits!

A HOST OF OTHER ATTRACTIONS

Two Big Stage Shows!

that's all–**ONE DIME!**–that's all

Calamity and asked her to join his "dime museum." His offer of $50 a week was too good to turn down. Calamity knew that most workers earned only a dollar a day. Her friends bought her a fancy buckskin suit. Ordered to wear highheeled boots, Calamity found she could barely walk in them.

The show opened in Minneapolis early in 1896. Large posters featured CALAMITY JANE, THE HEROINE OF A THOUSAND THRILLING ADVENTURES. Those who paid a dime found Calamity sitting on a raised platform. Polished six-shooters dangled from her hips. She greeted the crowd and told tall tales about the West. After the show, she sold copies of her life story.

Calamity preferred to tell her stories while relaxing in a saloon. Talking from a platform was hard for her. When she grew tired of being stared at, she took a few swigs of whiskey. Soon she was missing shows. Even though she was drawing big crowds, Middleton fired her.

In 1901, the Pan-American Exposition needed a headliner. Lured east by promises of star treatment, Calamity caught a train to Buffalo, New York. This time, management gave her a chance to show off. After a fanfare of bugle calls, she galloped into the center ring. Dressed in buckskins and heavily armed, she whooped and hollered and waved to the crowd. All agreed that Calamity had stolen the show.

After the show, Calamity went looking for more fun. Fortified with a few drinks, she took a team of horses for a drive. One account says that she shot up the fairgrounds.

After a final fling with the Pan-American Exposition of 1901, Calamity Jane returned to the West. This 1902 photo, taken in Montana, sums up the final years of her life. Drinking more heavily all the time, she wandered from place to place. Old friends pitched in to keep her fed and housed.

Another says she blackened the eye of a police officer. Calamity spent the night in jail, but that was nothing new. When she left, she handed out free show tickets to the police.

Calamity could not adjust to city life. When Buffalo Bill came by to visit, she poured out her woes: "Get me out of this rig," she begged. "It's got me thrown and tied. Give me the price of a free meal and a ticket to send me home."[5]

The odds are that Buffalo Bill did as she asked. He was at the height of his career. Calamity was on the way down.

9

"BURY ME NEXT TO WILD BILL"

Calamity returned to the Black Hills. In 1903, she was seen wandering from camp to camp. Old friends were saddened to see how she had aged. Her dark eyes stared out of a face burned brown by wind and sun. Her grin revealed just two yellow teeth. She was in her early fifties, but she looked seventy.[1] Heavy drinking was pushing her toward an early grave.

Early in July, she paid her final visit to Deadwood. Old friends paid her hotel bills. One of them drove her up to Wild Bill's grave. She posed there in her ragged black dress for one last photograph.

Calamity next showed up in Terry, eight miles from Deadwood. On August 1, she staggered into the Calloway Hotel. A maid put her to bed. A doctor was called, and friends gathered. Legend says she asked the date. Someone told her it was the second of August. The bad guess must have pleased Calamity. "Twenty-seventh anniversary of Wild Bill's murder," she whispered. "Be sure to bury me next to Wild Bill, ya hear?"[2] Moments later, she closed her eyes and died.

The Society of Black Hills Pioneers took charge of her funeral. At the church, masses of flowers nearly hid her coffin. A preacher talked about the time she nursed the sick and dying. He did not mention her drinking and hell-raising. A band played as a hearse carried her coffin to Mt. Moriah Cemetery. True to her last request, she was buried next to Wild Bill.

In 1903, Calamity looked about twenty years older than her actual age. In July, she paid her final visit to Deadwood and Wild Bill Hickok's grave. A month later, she staggered into the Calloway Hotel in nearby Terry. She died there that same day. Her friends in Deadwood honored her request to be buried next to Wild Bill.

For a time, it seemed as though Calamity had no more stories to tell. Then, on Mother's Day in 1941, newscaster Gabriel Heatter introduced grey-haired Jane Hickok McCormick. The woman told the radio audience that Calamity Jane and Wild Bill Hickok were her parents. As proof, she produced what she said was Calamity's diary. She also displayed a "wedding certificate" dated September 1, 1870. It was handwritten on a page torn from a Bible.

McCormick claimed that Calamity gave birth to her in a cave near Deadwood. Wild Bill, she said, abandoned his "wife" and daughter after the birth. Calamity, broke and forlorn, turned the infant over to an English couple. James O'Neill, captain of a Cunard Line steamship, raised little Jane as his own child. Calamity visited her only once, when she was eight, McCormick said.

Could all this be true? Research turns up many holes in the story. No one ever found the "Rev. Warren" who signed the wedding certificate. The Cunard Line never employed a Captain James O'Neill. Those who knew Calamity doubted that she kept a diary. The story is unlikely—but it might have happened.

Calamity lives on in films and novels. Hollywood's plots tend to play up her romances. In the 1937 film *The Plainsman,* Jean Arthur played Calamity to Gary Cooper's Wild Bill. Jane Russell had fun with the role in a 1948 comedy called *The Paleface.* Doris Day sang and danced the title role in the 1953 film *Calamity Jane.*

Television produced its own *Calamity Jane* in 1982. A

Today, Calamity Jane lives on in popular films and television shows. As with the early dime novels, Calamity would have laughed at the Hollywood version of her life. As a child of the Wild West, the natural beauty of this landmark near Custer, Montana, would have meant more to her. Survey maps identify the hill as Calamity Jane Horse Cache.

tough-as-nails Jane Alexander saves Wild Bill's life in an early scene. In 1995, television turned Larry McMurtry's novel *Buffalo Girls* into a mini-series. Anjelica Houston made a handsome Calamity Jane.

How would Calamity want to be remembered? She would have laughed out loud at seeing herself brought to life on the screen. The sight of the hill named for her in Montana would have delighted her. Watching tourists rush to buy her photograph would have been equally pleasing. In the end, she might have agreed with the writer who summed up her life in these words: "She swore, she drank, she wore men's clothing. She was just ahead of her time."[3]

CHAPTER NOTES

Chapter 1

1. Marthy Cannary Burke, *Life and Adventures of Calamity Jane by Herself* (Fairfield, Wash.: Ye Galleon Press, 1979), p. 5. Original edition published 1896.

2. Roberta Beed Sollid, *Calamity Jane: A Study in Historical Criticism* (Helena, Mont.: The Western Press, 1958), pp. 5–8.

3. Jesse Brown and A. M. Willard, *The Black Hills* (Rapid City, S.D.: The Rapid City Journal, 1924), pp. 412–413.

4. *Montana Post,* December 31, 1864 (Virginia City, Mont.).

5. Duncan Aikman, *Calamity Jane and the Lady Wildcats* (New York: Blue Ribbon Books, 1927), p. 44.

6. Watson Parker, *Deadwood: The Golden Years* (Lincoln, Neb.: University of Nebraska Press, 1981), p. 198.

7. Sollid, pp. 20–22.

Chapter 2

1. James D. Horan, *Desperate Women* (New York: Bonanza Books, 1952), p. 174.

2. Marthy Cannary Burke, *Life and Adventures of Calamity Jane by Herself* (Fairfield, Wash.: Ye Galleon Press, 1979), p. 5. Original edition published 1896.

3. Burke, p. 5.

4. *Montana Post,* December 31, 1864 (Virginia City, Mont.).

5. Burke, p. 6.

Chapter 3

1. James D. Horan, *Desperate Women* (New York: Bonanza Books, 1952), p. 176.

2. John S. McClintock, *Pioneer Days in the Black Hills* (Deadwood, S.D.: John S. McClintock, 1939), p. 116.

3. Marthy Cannary Burke, *Life and Adventures of Calamity Jane by Herself* (Fairfield, Wash.: Ye Galleon Press, 1979), pp. 6–7. Original edition published 1896.

4. Burke, p. 7–8.

5. Doris Faber, *Calamity Jane: Her Life and Her Legend* (Boston: Houghton Mifflin Company, 1992), p. 17.

6. Stewart H. Holbrook, *Little Annie Oakley and Other Rugged People* (New York: Macmillan, 1948), pp. 32–33.

7. Burke, p. 8.

Chapter 4

1. Glenn Clairmonte, *Calamity Was the Name for Jane* (Denver: Sage Books, 1959), pp. 118–119.

2. Marthy Cannary Burke, *Life and Adventures of Calamity Jane by Herself* (Fairfield, Wash.: Ye Galleon Press, 1979), p. 9. Original edition published 1896.

3. *Deadwood Pioneer,* July 13, 1876 (Deadwood, S.D.).

4. Burke, p. 10.

5. Joan S. Reiter, *The Old West: The Women* (Alexandria, Va.: Time-Life, 1978), p. 158.

Chapter 5

1. James D. Horan, *Desperate Women* (New York: Bonanza Books, 1952), p. 181.

2. Duncan Aikman, *Calamity Jane and the Lady Wildcats* (New York: Blue Ribbon Books, 1927), p. 107.

3. D. Dee, *Lowdown on Calamity Jane* (Rapid City, S.D., 1932), p. 4.

4. Horan, p. 182.

Chapter 6

1. Marthy Cannary Burke, *Life and Adventures of Calamity Jane by Herself* (Fairfield, Wash.: Ye Galleon Press, 1979), pp. 10–11. Original edition published 1896.

2. Duncan Aikman, *Calamity Jane and the Lady Wildcats* (New York: Blue Ribbon Books, 1927), p. 111.

3. James D. Horan, *Desperate Women* (New York: Bonanza Books, 1952), p. 185.

4. Burke, p. 11.

5. Aikman, pp. 113–114.

Chapter 7

1. Roberta Beed Sollid, *Calamity Jane: A Study in Historical Criticism* (Helena, Mont.: The Western Press, 1958), p. 13.

2. Edward L. Wheeler, "Deadwood Dick, the Prince of the Road; or, the Black Rider of the Black Hills," *Beadle's Half-Dime Library* (New York: Beadle and Adams, Publishers, 1877), reproduced in Everett Bleiler, ed., *Eight Dime Novels* (New York: Dover Publications, 1974), p. 88.

3. *Avant Courier,* August 7, 1903 (Bozeman, Mont.).

4. Dee Brown, *Wondrous Times on the Frontier* (Little Rock, Ark.: August House Publishers, 1991), p. 157.

5. James D. Horan, *Desperate Women* (New York: Bonanza Books, 1952), p. 186.

Chapter 8

1. Glenn Clairmonte, *Calamity Was the Name for Jane* (Denver: Sage Books, 1959), pp. 189–190.

2. J. Leonard Jennewein, *Calamity Jane of the Western Trails* (Huron, S.D.: Dakota Books, 1953), p. 29.

3. *The Lead Call,* November 9, 1895 (Deadwood, S.D.).

4. Ellen Crago Moeller, *Calamity Jane* (Laramie, Wyo.: Jelm Mountain Press, 1981), p. 18.

5. James D. Horan, *Desperate Women* (New York: Bonanza Books, 1952), p. 192.

Chapter 9

1. James D. Horan, *Desperate Women* (New York: Bonanza Books, 1952), pp. 192–193.

2. Glenn Clairmonte, *Calamity Was the Name for Jane* (Denver: Sage Books, 1959), pp. 210–211.

3. Quoted in Doris Faber, *Calamity Jane: Her Life and Her Legend* (Boston: Houghton Mifflin Company, 1992), p. 49.

GLOSSARY

assassin—A murderer; someone who kills a well-known person.

bandanna—A large, brightly-colored handkerchief that cowboys often wore around their necks. Worn over the nose and mouth, it filtered out the dust raised by ox teams.

buckskins—Pants and jackets made from the tanned hide of a male deer.

bullwacker—The driver of a team of oxen. Bullwackers were known for their skillful use of twenty-foot rawhide whips.

calamity—An event that brings a severe loss or causes distress; a disaster.

dime novels—Low-cost magazines that printed popular fiction during the late 1800s.

dispatch—Official message that the sender wants delivered as quickly as possible.

frontier—A region just being opened to settlers.

gold dust—Small flakes of gold, usually found by panning in streams. In the Wild West, gold dust was often used in place of money.

midwife—A woman who helps in childbirth. In the Wild West, midwives seldom had formal medical training.

pockmark—A small, round scar. In the Wild West, smallpox and chicken pox often left pockmarks in the skin of the survivors.

prospector—Someone who searches for gold or other mineral deposits.

quicksand—A bed of soft, loose sand, often in a riverbed, that cannot hold a person or animal's weight.

rodeo—An exhibition of cowboy skills. Rodeo events include riding and roping competitions.

scout—A skilled tracker and guide who rides ahead of a group to gather information about the land and dangers that lie ahead.

Stetson—A popular brand of cowboy hats.

tenderfoot—A newcomer to the West.

wagon tongue—The pole that is attached to the front axle of a wagon. Horses, mules, and oxen are harnassed to the wagon tongue.

MORE GOOD READING ABOUT
CALAMITY JANE

Aikman, Duncan. *Calamity Jane and the Lady Wildcats.* New York: Blue Ribbon Books, 1927.

Burke, Marthy Cannary. *Life and Adventures of Calamity Jane by Herself.* Fairfield, Wash.: Ye Galleon Press, 1979. Original edition published 1896.

Clairmonte, Glenn. *Calamity Was the Name for Jane.* Denver: Sage Books, 1959.

Faber, Doris. *Calamity Jane: Her Life and Her Legend.* Boston: Houghton Mifflin Company, 1992.

Horan, James D. *Desperate Women.* New York: Bonanza Books, 1952.

Moeller, Ellen Crago. *Calamity Jane.* Laramie, Wyo.: Jelm Mountain Press, 1981.

Sollid, Roberta Beed. *Calamity Jane: A Study in Historical Criticism.* Helena, Mont.: The Western Press, 1958.

INDEX